TAKE WHAT YOU WANT

TAKE WHAT YOU WANT

Henrietta Goodman

ALICE JAMES BOOKS
FARMINGTON, MAINE

10 9 8 7 6 5 4 3 2 1

Alice James Books are published by Alice James Poetry Cooperative, Inc.,
an affiliate of the University of Maine at Farmington.

ALICE JAMES BOOKS
238 MAIN STREET
FARMINGTON, ME 04938

www.alicejamesbooks.org

Library of Congress Cataloging-in-Publication Data
Goodman, Henrietta, 1970-
 Take what you want / Henrietta Goodman.
  p. cm.
 ISBN-13: 978-1-882295-62-3
 ISBN-10: 1-882295-62-5
 I. Title.

 PS3607.O568T35 2007
 811'.6--DC22

              2007001417

Alice James Books gratefully acknowledges support from the University
of Maine at Farmington and the National Endowment for the Arts. ❦

Cover Art: Ford Maddox Brown, *Mauvais Sujet*,
1863, Watercolour on paper, 232 x 210 mm.
Photograph © Tate Gallery, London / Art Resource, NY.

ACKNOWLEDGEMENTS

Grateful acknowledgement is made to the editors of the following journals, in which some of these poems first appeared (sometimes in slightly different forms):

Alkali Flats: "Bear #1"
Fine Madness: "Confessional with Stipulations"
Hubbub: "Physics," "Suture," "Paradise," "Pet Names"
Main Street Rag: "Truckstop Elegy," "Bear #2"
Mid-American Review: "Ars Poetica"
NEO: "Farewell Note in Czech," "Madrones," "Gretel," "Descent," "Negatives"
North Carolina Literary Review: "Red Poppy," "At the Bridge"
Northwest Review: "Signs"
RUNES, A Review of Poetry: "Colonization"
Southern Poetry Review: "Trees near Water"
Teacup: "Silk Trick"
Willow Springs: "Reproduction"

I would like to thank the Montana Arts Council for its generous support in the form of an Individual Artist Fellowship, and Bradley and Frank Boyden for allowing me to attend the Marjorie Davis Boyden Wilderness Writing Residency, an experience that shaped many of the poems in this book. I am also grateful for the inspiration, insight and support provided by Kevin Goodan, Chelsey Robison, and Nate Schneider.

for my sons,
Cole and Scott

CONTENTS

I.

II.

III.

IV.

I.

SILK TRICK

The man at the door
has plucked and cleaned
a pheasant. He offers it
to me, his hands smeared
with blood and feathers.
Today my scars hardly show.
When he asks my name
I say *Vanessa.*
I wedge the back of a chair
under the doorknob
and hang blankets
over the windows.
I have two beds. I take him
to the one for sleeping alone
but I lie down beside him.

In the morning he wants me
to tell stories.
How will you know
what's true, I ask.
I uncrumple my piece
of red silk. It flutters,
nearly transparent.
I make it vanish and reappear.
He asks where I learned how.
I tell him I can't
remember. He grabs
my hands. I don't know
if he's the same man
as last night.

His eyes are darker.
The house is quiet.
Every now and then the clock
skips. He turns his face
against my palm.
What are these days called,
these days I can't find
on the calendar?

GRACE

Those two on the couch,
        paperback copy of the Kama Sutra
             spread open across their knees,
   what do they know about it?
What does anyone know?
      My friend Sarah says to dance is to fall
   a thousand times, and I am thinking
            of that, thinking of you
last spring on the kite flats, stepping backward,
               the kite swooping
      and dipping, diving like a bird
bent on entering the ground—
    you, running, the spool unwound,
         the orange and blue kite caught
   in a downdraft, then finally flying steady,
a swimmer beyond the waves.
      Sarah says someone is watching us dance,
   a stern instructor who loves his students,
    and someone else calls him Gepetto,
an old bastard with strings
         and crossed sticks, like you
  with the kite,
     or was it the kite, with you?
Or is there no difference, after all,
         if we find grace by falling?

PARADISE

Outside the Dixon General Store,
Kevin and I eat fried fruit pies.
Sundays, the Dixon Bar is closed.
Across the bridge, Paradise,
population 300. I am not thinking
what paradise could mean as the striped cliffs
lead us in. The green river matches
the green of the sky in the east—
what is hail in Paradise?
Ice, like anywhere else.
Kevin says, *I could live here.*
Paradise has two bars, both open.
If I were Kevin, this poem might be about irony.
He would tell me: *You should have left*
that deer skull where you found it
instead of taking it to Paradise
in a paper bag on the seat between us.
He might try to make me tell him
why I wanted it. I could make up
something good enough
about the permanence of bone.
It would be worse to take it
and then put it back,
he'd say. I almost forgot
this is not Kevin's poem.
Never mind the deer skull. Go back
to Paradise. I drive fast, faster.
He says we might reach escape velocity.
We talk about what would happen.

THE SKY IS WHITE
AND THE EARTH IS FLAT

On the edge of town, the junkyard bears
its rusted crop in alphabetized rows.
I lug his toolbox through the rutted field
of knapweed and bees, little squares
of glass crunching as the sun lowers
upon us. I am careful where I step
since likeness tricks two ways, or three—
first as artifice, which is easy:
Ford transmission=phonograph horn=trumpet flower
second as simple mistake:
not snake but coil of fuel line, harmless as shed skin
or worse, as love:
just light off a shard of tarnished mirror
and like crows we are drawn down,
half-mad and cawing.

GRETEL RECONSIDERS

It's true we were abandoned,
though I was older. My parents
were ignorance, propriety.
His were faith. I treated him
like a child at first, praised
his art, refused to let him pay.
I laughed at his uncombed hair,
the bits of leaves stuck to his clothes.
Later, I gave him my key.

We wandered until we found
one room that belonged only to us,
one narrow bed, one window.
Always, it was night, always winter,
snow blowing sideways under
the streetlight, the woman
in the next room cursing
her children, an echo of crying,
of an open hand on skin. Always
we were naked but never innocent.
What did we think would happen?
The trail diverges here, dissolves.
We were not so different
from our parents after all—
so greedy, so willing to yield.

RED POPPY

The possibilities are not
endless. It's summer:
around our heads,
a swarm of intentions…
no-see-ums, let's say.

Beyond potential lies choice—
a white room, Georgia O'Keeffe prints
on the ceiling, a quarter-cup
of blood in a tube.

Is it true what they say
about Georgia O'Keeffe?
If so, the vagina is widespread,
meaning, pardon me, everywhere:
waiting rooms, galleries,
the walls of subways and buses.

I'm in red silk panties
that tie in a knot at each hip.
Nothing can be rectified.
We don't know that we already know this.
We're on the floor, a coil
of extension cord
under my spine.
I don't feel it now. I'll feel it
later. Meaning, as they say,
you can't change your mind
after this. Music's playing,
feedback and garbled speech,

a guitar like a sword
through a sheet.

Possibility is an ocean
that tastes like you.
I don't think I have it backward.
Is it true what they say?
I close my eyes. I see an afterimage,
a bright light,
a red poppy with oblivion
at its center.

SVEN LOVES DANGER

According to the wall along the freeway
near Drummond, Sven loves danger. On the broad
shoulders of his best friend, flashlight in his teeth,

he sprays the words in a cherry-red mist
that blows back to speckle his face. Sven
loves danger, and all the girls love him best,

the ones who want to save him and the ones
who think if they can't have him, they can
be him, as if Sven, at seventeen, is temptation

itself, leading them into bars and fast rivers
and the cars of strangers, into the arms of men
whose faces they forget when the light

is out, whose fingers leave no trace—
when what they want is the indelible declaration,
risk and its corollary, its claim.

SNOW AT GIVERNY

Halfway through the description of the room,
she knows she is mapping her own
mysterious ancestry. In other people's rooms
the background blues and greens of pictures
atop a black piano are not proof of predeterminism;
the artificial fire flaring pallid orange
to the sound of gears is only tacky,
not another inscrutable clue.

She wants anonymous department store
furnishings, unsullied by the accumulation
of foiled intention: cheap new chairs,
cheap new drapes, a canvas of bland impressionist dots
that resolve at the proper distance
into a simple garden—

not that lamp with the frosted
blown-glass shade, those small, hard pillows,
not the portrait of that ancient child
with androgynous ringlets
and a white smock.

She wants the proper distance,
any Monet but the white expanse of *Snow at Giverny*—
more luminous, bluer, the farther she backs away
until she can't tell if the air is on fire or frozen—
one more flame she can't quench and can't feed.

STEVENSVILLE

The asphalt under my bare feet is body
temperature, smooth and damp. A band

plays on the back of a flatbed truck,
lit by red and blue floodlights. The purple

light on the drummer's arms matches
the sky where the sun has set into a bank

of clouds, so he can look into it
like a mirror and see where he is not.

Static cracks in his microphone, in the tangle
of wires that connects him to the rest

of the band. I love him for nothing more
than this: for singing these sad songs

like they are true, like he's looking not
into the sky, but into my own past, or future.

RED BERRIES

I wake and say *mama*. I don't know
if I am calling her. Overnight
the berries turned from orange
to red. *What does my back feel like?*
he asks. All week two fish swim circles
in the washtub. When I release them
at the reservoir, clay pigeons shatter.
The shots send tremors through the water.
Like moths, the fish refuse to leave
my hands. They want to fly in my hair.

My mother types, sucking a penny.
I sit on the floor by her desk. Now
I'll confess: I cracked the lightbulbs.
It was after I fell in love. *My pearl,*
she says, *you can't escape politics.*
This isn't the scene I wanted. A man
stands by a rock wall. He is tired
of walking. He takes off his pack.
My mother shows me the black hairs
on her breasts.

ORPHEUS, EURYDICE...

How sick I am of empiricism.
Must we be like them?

A woman
hears a noise
in the night and stands,
hand on the knob. God,

it's so predictable, the audience
screaming *don't open the door—*

Imagine her arrogance,
stepping onto the porch:
the glow of her flashlight,
the vast, greedy dark.

II.

TRUCKSTOP ELEGY

I'm back at the truckstop. The man
with me tonight writes his name in the snow
on the hood of a green Mercedes.
Driving down the long hill,
I ate grapes from his hand.
Sometimes when I reached without looking,
I took hold of his fingers instead.
A waitress stands by our table,
her silence broken by engines idling,
trucks gearing up or down. She adjusts
the pink carnation in her buttonhole.
I can't decide what I want.

At midnight, a little boy drops a coin
into the saddlebag of a mechanical donkey.
I call the music it plays *Truckstop Elegy*
because it sounds so hollow, like a beehive,
a rotten log, like the buzzing in my lips
after a kiss. In the gift shop the man
spins a postcard rack until dust swims,
paramecia in florescent light.
He wants to kiss me again. I walk back
to our table and pick up the phone. I dial
my own number just to hear it ring.

GRETEL

In one version, the witch wins.
What lesson in that, besides we get
what we do not deserve? Cast out
to follow a distant curl of smoke,
we leave our past behind
and find our way, or don't.
That smoke might come not from
a chimney but the forest on fire—
trees exploding, a column
of flame two hundred feet high.
Take off your leather coat,
brother, and let me put my hands
against your chest. Even if we stop
in the middle of the story
and set out alone over these acres
of scorched earth filling up
with more water than the sky can hold—
still beyond us that curl of smoke
that who'd blame us
if we mistook for home?

FLOODPLAIN

This is your world, your words,
not mine, not lies but versions:
sweetgum tree, green flies
walking on water, hellgrammites
stuck to river rock, prehistoric
casings. We're in the floodplain,
among the bedraggled willows
of spring runoff, a dust of silt
over rocks, grass, an unkept house.

Nothing here's going to answer
my questions. Amid the swell
and sink of flood, you sit speechless,
thinking only of assimilation,
the plow, thistle of the mind,
gristle of meat. A stick of kindling
splinters across your back, your father
boots your ass up the attic stairs—
all the furniture under sheets,
coil of rope, phonograph, photo
of the uncle who lost one leg,
then the other, ancient mirror.

CONFESSIONAL
WITH STIPULATIONS

The cottonwoods smell, as you say, like a millipede pulled into pieces.

One apple still clings to the tree, weightless, hollow at the core, abandoned even by bees.

He brought a basket of shells all the way from the ocean, each one bone-white, each one, of course, empty.

Driving toward Wisdom at night, in winter, we took off our clothes.

Snow swirled like a whirlpool, like a dervish.

Most days Wisdom is the coldest place in the country. Wisdom says *don't count on it*. We should have dressed in layers. We should have kept them on.

The word *baby* is sexy, especially in a sentence like *Baby, I don't know*.

We took off our clothes and swam in a strange river with a secret cave beneath the water.

We all know what that means.

My house filled with people. They pressed their faces to the windows, lined up like a chorus on the stairs. I had to confess: *I love him so much*, I said.

Don't count on it.

Coming out of anesthesia all I could do was cry. This is normal.
Men throw up. Women cry. *Henry*, I cried, *Henry*—

A lost dog licked my hand.

I had to prove it, but not to him, already gone, a ghost burning
papers in the basement, hands held over the small green flame.

DESCENT

I am wearing a new black leather belt
with two rows of silver spikes

and you are wearing a new pair
of wool gloves with a red heart

sewn badly on the inside of each wrist
and we are walking in the snow,

stopping while you undo the flap
that covers your fingers and cup your hand

around the flame of your lighter,
and I am watching the hollow

of your cheek as you breathe smoke,
gestures I should not love, but love,

and I am thinking of the downdraft
of snow through the grated ceiling

of the underpass north of town,
a powder fine as frozen steam,

and of how as a little girl I dreamed
again and again of my descent

into hell—the red glow like a hand
cupped around a flashlight,

like a flashlight held beneath a face
in the heavy dark of a canvas tent:

I am thinking of the magnetic pull of pain
to pain, thinking *know me, know me, know me.*

SIGNS

The choice had more to do
with waiting than I thought.
I built a fire at the edge
of the field and burned my dress
as airplane lights washed over me.
While I drove he burned
my list of numbers in the ashtray.
On the other side of the pass,
he changed the clock.
He put a bottle cap
under the broken wiper.
The scraping stopped. Snow fell
straight down. This was one
option. I couldn't think
of the other.

GRETEL ALONE

Call these woods a cage and you wouldn't
be so far wrong—sun long gone
by late afternoon and town farther.

Trees fall for no reason, just their own weight
pulling them moaning down. I keep a list
of untraceable sound: a giggle of water,

a drum, something, or someone, bawling.
Beyond the meadow, nothing but thornbrush
and a bad smell. Who taught me these rules—

don't walk in the white fog that fills
the valley and rises like a smothering
dough. Don't touch the white foam

that bubbles from certain plants like the mouth
of a rabid dog. Whose whisper says build
a necklace from the bleached spine of a bird,

the hollow globe of a wasp gall, smooth
and weightless, but stringed inside? A woman
in an alley puts her hand through the dark

of a barred window and stands still a long
time. A child holds the woman's free hand,
red candy plugging her mouth, the tall window

empty as a blind eye. I walk the trail
to the river with a metal rake, peeling back

layers of moss and leaves. I snag vines

and tear them free, roll rocks to the edge
and push them over. Do I mean to preserve
the trail or obscure it, as I step backward

in a cloud of stinging gnats, erasing
my footprints as I go? In a breeze a rain
of needles falls. I am half a story.

TREES NEAR WATER

To get this right I need to know more
about trees near water. Most of what I've heard
concerns their weak vascular systems,

blurred growth rings, weak hearts.
I've heard good things can grow
from bad soil. I need to know the intentions

of the couple in the car at the water's edge,
the aphrodisiac properties of weather,
the clouds that pile like so many bodies

in hard pursuit of each other. I need to know
what he says to her just before they kiss,
whether the trees are aspen, cottonwood,

birch, whether their leaves have turned
belly-up in wind. The kiss itself
doesn't matter—it's what comes before

that drives them straight into the storm,
the horse rearing up against a fence
lined with purple and gold iris,

the white flash of that horse's eye,
starlings bobbing on a black wire.
I need to hear the song that's playing

through bursts of static. All I know so far
is what that song wants to do. It wants

to strike you. It wants to give you

your own pain like a gift and make you
glad to take it. It's in accord with the tornado
forming above the fields on the other side

of the river. It wants you to forsake
all others and take this twisting dark body
in your arms and dance.

BEAR #1

In my long sleeps the roads all turn
to rivers. The sun moves behind
brown clouds in a sky full of crows
and yellow leaves, the smell
of rotting fruit. I search for patterns
in frost on the windows while my husband
waits in the blind, his legs and back
grown stiff. He carries baskets of windfall
from the orchard to the flattened grass
at the base of the cliff and the bear
keeps coming back. I can't decide
if it's better to have too much
or too little faith. I struggle upstream,
over slippery rocks. The bear begs
for just one kiss and I always give it.
My hands sink into the thick black
fur and never reach skin.

BEAR #2

Tonight we lie by the fire
on a black bearskin. The fur
absorbs the muted light,
the heat. I've called this
a pleasure, but how do I know?
What if in your sleep the dead
weight of the bear still drapes
across your shoulders
as you head through the trees
for home? Is it too heavy?
Is it heavy enough?

THE DOOR OPENS

The door opens to red drops
like balls of mercury,
bag of fishheads in the kitchen,
scrutiny of each gelled eye.

You won't remember any of this:
monotony of water, mutter of TV.
Blue pills rattle on hardwood.
In the mirror I hold your face still.

Doesn't it hurt to finally tell
the truth, tooth broken at the root,
hole through the center
of your tongue?

You rinse with beer and spit more blood.
Who did this I say and you say *men.*

III.

AT THE BRIDGE

The baby is four days old
and I am running along the river
at dusk, stitched together,
bleeding. Like a shell
the body opens and the baby
emerges, Botticelli's Venus—
ears flat disks no larger
than nickels, fingers blanched
and wrinkled, larval.
In the tunnel, the faint smell
of something burned or burning
echos on the steel walls.
My feet disturb the path.
How long can I last,
unhinged? Someone has a doll
shaped like me. Someone
is pushing in pins. A baby cries
in the willow thicket
and a white bird rises, eyes me
and cries again, fish bent
in its curved beak. At the bridge
I run between two angry girls.
One yells *you better find it*
or I'll kick your ass—
and the other stares
me down as if I have it,
whatever it is.

ARS POETICA

Why do we think we have any control
at all? My breasts are soggy cartons.
The baby is greedy. He grabs
my skin in his fists, twists my hair.
He seems to know everything
already, the checkbook, balanced wrong,
the ignorance I'm not supposed
to confess—my friend says *Giotto*
and I hear *Choteau*, tiny town not far
from here. Clearly, I can imagine
no farther. The valley's a funnel,

skyline blurred by charcoal clouds,
the valley's a tornado and I'm
the eye—*doodlebug, doodlebug
your house is on fire*—
the room spins and spins
until the floor drops away
and I'm dizzy, frescoed to the wall,
Madonna Defying Gravity.
You can't tell it yet,
but I'm slipping, scratching the days
in my skin with a dull blade,
too afraid to just cut clean
and deep. This is how prisoners do it,

one scratch for each day
on the wall that holds them in,
one for each day I've lost
in half-sleep, the baby curled

like a snail on my chest, my hand patting,
patting, stomach bulging
over the top of my pants—

what is restrained in one place
escapes in another—

PET NAMES

We wake to a day so flat
the mountains look painted
on the sky. No way they could hold
a winter's worth of snow.
No way we're far from home.
Home is the next page,
paper-thin. This is the astigmatic
view, a pale sky with no clouds
to show how close or far away
we are. This is a picture of a car.
Put on your 3-D glasses.
This is a picture of us
wearing 3-D glasses.
My husband wants me
to call him by a pet name.
I call him Sweetie,
but only when I'm being condescending.
When we talk to the baby
we speak of ourselves
in the third person.
I say *Mommy's sorry,*
Mommy's sorry, Mommy's sorry.
What's your pet name
for the fourth dimension?
I call it river of sorrow.
In red letters, my t-shirt says
It seemed like a good idea
at the time. What I really want
to know is, who is the fourth person?
We drive all day.
We don't get anywhere.

AN APOLOGY

Along the stone walls
the calla lilies
have each begun to unfold
one white sheet
freckled with pollen,
and I have begun to envy them.
Last night I watched a girl
across the street catch fireflies
in her cupped hands
and smear their light
along the wall
in phosphorescent streaks.
She wrote her name,
or someone's.
How could she not
remind you of me,
her cruelty so irrelevant,
so intent on preservation?

SUTURE

The motel ceiling glitters
like asphalt when the light is out—
little mirror chips,
a disco ball over this dirty bed.
We sleep on the bleached towels,
the baby between us. How far
to the nearest ocean?
How to tell the true oasis
from the shimmer of witch-water,
the mirage that leaps electrically
from hill to hill, always ahead?
If we lie here long enough
we could make constellations
from the specks on the ceiling.
We could make order from chaos,
the same way we call that cloud
a heron, and that one a deer,
or a door. The smell of a diesel
engine left to idle fills the room.
I remember the bloodstain
on the highway we passed over.
The suture between two
clouds dissolves.

GRETEL AND THE BAT

All that's left:
a residue of dread,
a woman alone

at night in a cabin
in a clearing. No evil here,
just a small black hole,
the roving vibration

of a moth unseduced
by light. She wakes

to a determined chirping,
the scrabbling of claws
on glass. Fixed,

finally, in the beam
of her lamp—
gray frog, plucked bird—
it gutters

then clambers through a slit
in the screen
as if it has known all along

the way out. She wakes
to sun and a swarm

of hummingbirds.
No evil here.

But all day she covers

her head as she waits
for the walls to shuffle
like cards
and the black queen
to flutter down.

A SUDDEN FALLING

This was the summer we had the baby,
the summer I saw as the end of all
but the domestic—ritual and boring,

not worth the bother of words.
This was the summer my aunt sent
clippings from the paper,

the Cape Hatteras lighthouse
moved safely out of ocean's reach,
workers tossing their hats in the air.

On the phone, a woman told me
having a baby made her afraid of dying,
made her reconsider riding drunk

on the back of a motorcycle at two A.M.
This was the summer we lived
half a block from the tracks,

when the Mexican railroad killer
eluded capture for the baby's whole
first month, so I had something almost

real to fear as I pushed the stroller
through the park at dusk, or ran
up the big hill, trying to leave behind

the smells of sour milk and sweat.
When he allowed himself to be caught

on a bridge on the border and confessed

in court in Spanish, his voice on the radio
was so soft, so strangely beautiful
that I heard it more in my body

than my ears, the way I felt the baby
move before he was born—a sudden
falling, the jerk of a foot, or a hand.

MOTHER

What would my mother say,
if she heard me talking like this?
You should be ashamed
of yourself, people will think
you don't love the baby—
But look, I can show you:

the hottest night of the year,
I lay him down, star on the midnight
sheet, unsnap the snaps, take off
the shirt, the diaper. Luminescent,
toothless, seven weeks old, he grins
as I fan him up and down, back
and forth with my Chinese fan,
unfurls his arms and legs
under the butterflies
and the bright silk flowers.

PHYSICS

Psychology takes the fun
out of everything, and infinity
can only be fathomed
as infinite boredom
or infinite loss.
Physics, which we used to trust,
fails us altogether when the number 8
turned on its side
turns out to be merely sleeping—
rises up like a cow in a field,
a cow with surprising vigor.

His hand tangles in my hair
as the train passes,
and in that blur of sound and light
things are settled by a force
outside ourselves,
as we had hoped would happen.
In the afternoon,
the green plums hang invisible
on the green tree. At night they glow
with a powdery green light of their own—
sour enough to last a while,
sour enough, surely.

RIVER ONTO RIVER

The baby has grown out of his newborn
clothes. He clamps my nipple in his gums
and tugs, shakes his head like a dog

with a bone. The day the mountain caught fire,
my husband stood in the street and watched
the plume of smoke grow, the red eye

of flame open. He held the baby up and pointed
as the small plane circled and the larger
plane followed, spilling water sucked up

from the river, spraying orange retardant,
orange foam onto orange flame, river onto
river. The burned spot remains

in the shape of an angel, black heart
of folded wings, black halo. My husband
points at her too, while I am kissing

the baby's cheek and trimming
his fingernails with my teeth and licking
the bitter taste of wax from the whorls

of his ear without wondering if these are strange
things to do. The baby grabs my hair
and says *quoi*. He will have teeth soon.
He still cries without tears.

MADRONES

There are trees here that shed
their bark every year. They're doing it
now, in wine-colored strips
that peel back as if burst
from within.
The new surface covers nothing.
It's just a border,
an intimacy of tree
and air:

each bare limb smooth
and hard, unstrippable
beyond this
without ruin.

Where is that point in me,
in you?
What must it be like to know,
to be so open,
so at home in the world?

GRETEL IN THE TUNNEL

Brother, why must we enter?
The mountain opens—in the night,
a blacker hole. My shoes twist
on gravel. This is the mouth
of the monster in every dream:
black teeth, the smell of rotten leaves.

No light at the end. Without touching the walls,
how will we know where the path bends?
Is this a lesson—your gentle taunts,
not-quite-hidden exasperation? Nothing to be afraid of,
unless you're afraid of *nothing*—this hole
could devour us, press us flat, eyeless,
like the fish that live deep in caves.
At whose mercy are we?

When we reach the threshold
I want to be carried out into the lighter dark,
because, truly, I have given myself to you.
Without you I would run, panicked, headlong.
Without you I wouldn't be here at all.

And when you sit on a rock under
the blurry moon to rub the marks
of my nails from your arm—
don't you know the only way home
is to go back through? What will I make
of the gift you offered, that I could not accept
and could not refuse?

NEGATIVES

Today I'm a wife. Today I'm a wife
and someone is dead and someone else

is dying. On the cracked plateau
I've got flowers where my fingers

should be, olive branches at my ankles.
The road rises on an ocean of grass,

the Snake river a bloated worm below.
Death is so easy to appropriate—

the dead belong to whoever wants
to use them, like Wanda's Puppets

in the yellow house outside of Anatone.
In the negatives my dress will look

black, our faces somber, squinting
into the hypodermic sun. We go

through the motions. We go on
making promises as if they could keep us.

We melt like butter. By night we're
Husband, Wife. Solid again, but changed.

IV.

SWALLOWS

It's hard to tell the true morel from the false—
that melting shape, surface like a cliff
full of holes where swallows
circle in and out, where they swarm
in the orderless logic of the flock.
We hike a trail as steep as the dream
in which gravity proves itself.

He wants to lace his fingers through
mine, to walk through a frost-covered field
under a pure white sky. He wants

this specific happiness to cancel
all recall of what came before.
Outside our bedroom window,
an owl asks *who-who, who-who?*
You're mine, mine, I say in a greedy
rush, like Rumpelstiltskin
stamping the floor

until all the objects come to life,
a blizzard of swirling dust—
straw or gold, we can't stop
sneezing. *Help,* screams the clock,
draped languidly over the rearing bed,
help, I'm being stolen, I'm being borne away—

REPRODUCTION

On the street, a crow
tears at the throat of a dead
pigeon. It eyes me sideways
and bobs a little, gray feathers
and a bit of red flesh hanging
from its beak. Its throat
moves; it swallows, bouncing
like a child listening
to music, like my own son
playing his cowboy songs,
Polly Wolly Doodle and *Buffalo Gals*—
hair like dandelion fluff,
thumb in his mouth, bouncing
a little from the knees.

DAMAGE

Almost three years ago on the balcony
I looked down and saw a row
of thick black stitches
disappearing under your cutoff
jeans. When I asked, you showed me
the tattoo that twisted up
from your ankle around your leg,
up your back and down your forearm—
a vine, you said, but I saw
that this vine, if it were real,
would be wire, with thorns,
or barbs. I was right, after all—
it was meant to suggest you had been torn
apart and put back together. No matter
what you said, leaning so calmly
against the rail, you were another
who believed yourself forged by damage.
That warm summer night,
my son asleep in his car seat,
my husband yawning, too polite
to tell me it was time to leave,
it didn't matter what you said—
you'd show it all to me later.

UNFAITHFUL PASTORAL

This is all going to go away—
sound of water in the half-frozen creek,
sound of wings. The crows will stop
laughing. Right now I'm going to sit
here and try to forget I'm part
of a long tradition.

Near an old foundation, a sheet
of metal rusts to red lace. Two white
horses gallop through patches of snow
to the edge of the meadow and stop.
I remember what the man
driving his truck through the tall grass
told us weeks ago—
they're their own horses.

Identical except for the black bird landing
on the back of one, they won't
let anyone near them, not the hunters
who bring them loads of hay,
not even us, walking up as close
as we can, small apples
in our outstretched hands.

TRANSPARENCY

The problem is, we only see part
of the problem. We see the hole
punched in the wall. We see the woman
who is not crying, though she knows
she should. There is the life we dreamed
together, and here is the one we will have
instead, in which we simply overlap.
In the quiet building at 5 P.M., a woman
sits on a desk with her legs spread,
and the man who stands between them
is the one who thinks he loves her,
not the one who loves the woman
he thinks she is. Stray images trail
like toilet paper on the bottom of a shoe—
the whole mess of what everyone wants
and wants to give away. Keep this,
this picture of a girl in cat-eye glasses
and a black v-necked dress, a man
in a cowboy hat standing beside her
on the street in early evening.
Each picture is a trap—
here you were when you loved
this man, and here you were when—
and here you are, caught by what you know
you felt, as though the mere fact
of the frozen image means you can never
have it back—to look on, yes,
but not to look out from.

CUTTING OUT HEARTS

My son wants to know why red
is a valentine color and I say
because hearts are red,
but everyone knows the heart
looks nothing like these symmetrical
paper shapes—the heart
a clenched fist, out to protect
itself, out to continue
its simple iambic job. To lie
with my head on your chest—
nothing beats it, even though I know
all I hear is an ugly clock,
a sturdy machine as full
of blood as a tick on a dog.
I want to stay with you, I say,
as if the heart hears anything
at all, as if it is flattered
by my good imitation.
You broke my heart, I say,
but to the heart there's no difference
between love and the dark street
where I walk alone, hands closed
into fists, thumb on the outside
like any good fighter.
To the heart there's no difference
between love and a cigarette—

WIND AND MORE WIND

On the boardwalk, men sink traps
full of yellow fat. Shirtless, skin
like brick, they pretend not to hear
as we bait each other. My son
pokes a stick in the sand.
A knot of fiddler crabs untangles
to brandish their claws, tiny
Don Quixotes. All day a storm
blows toward us. I walk under
the sea oaks waiting for the crack
and crash, a tangible threat,
not your hands that would never
hurt me. I want to sink into soft
wet sand, nothing left on the surface
but a small hole, an occasional
string of bubbles.

SO YOU SEE

I.
So you see how I spend
my days. Comforted
by the electric hum of insects.

Comforted by the planes that pass over.
I call out to each one—
Rapunzel, Rapunzel—
picture a knotted rope
dropping through layers of cloud,
uncloud, cloud:

hair of the world, dreadlock
of civilization, one strand
of one braid brushes my face.

II.
My son says *Mommy, I want
to keep you safe.*
He pushes a stroller
through the cabin, crashing
into walls, the doll slumped and naked.

He shoots me with his pistol,
says *You're dead, you're dead.*
Some days I believe him.
He has to pry my lids open.
I dream of how I'll return,
how I'll have to sit
on my hands.

III.
Or like this: empirical,
because I know nothing
in advance. When I praised
the madrone for stripping
so perfectly bare, this tree was more
performer than I imagined—
always something hidden,
kept sacred, safe.

Now this new layer appears—
pistachio, lime, chartreuse—
is this all? I think of the smugglers' trick,
the real canvas buried
beneath layers of amateur paint.
I am gullible
and know nothing
except how to wait.

NO ONE IS DEAD

Should I have said *lately*,
or *at least*? I am trying to console
myself. We all know the world
is built on the dead—
everything we touch,
maybe even we ourselves—

first love, underground;
father, underground;
child of Cindy and Joe,
former owners of this house,
child for whom the bathroom grew
to hold a wheelchair, giant
tiled shower, empty box
of Depends left in a cupboard,
underground.

Cindy gets a postcard
every month from Healing Hearts
for Moms, and if one of these cards
lies unforwarded in the tin tunnel
of the mailbox with the early bee
I trapped one May afternoon,
too cold to fly, what does that say?

And when I open the box
and find nothing but the card
and the bee, sluggish in the sudden
sun, then suddenly birthed
from the dark door
straight into my face—

can I use the words *angry resurrection?*
Can I say no one is dead
and call this reason enough
for sorrow?

HOMECOMING

My mother says *at least he doesn't hit you*—
The rest is familiar: whale-shaped spot
on the bathroom wall, glue traps full of spiders,
the smell of rotting apples and Raid. Kudzu
grows layer over layer like strips of paper mache
on the frames of trees. Feelers of ivy creep
over the sidewalk, my aunt salts the grass
that grows in cracks, and no one tells any secrets.
At the end of the street, frayed ribbon wraps
a tree, the scar on the trunk beginning to heal.
This is the scene of head-on, of unlawful commerce,
of renters. This is the house, still empty, red mud
splashed on white paint, faint lemon-smell
of the magnolia's waxy blossoms. If you didn't
know, you wouldn't know about the seeds inside
the brown cones, shiny as nail polish, red as lava.
This is how it is around here—no noise, no scandal.
Red seeds inside the brown cones, but no eruption.

FAREWELL NOTE IN CZECH

This is only what is always left—
a language you can't read,
tiny sketch of far-off mountains.

The words you know are *love* and *goodbye*
and you don't want to translate the rest.
It's enough to hold
the sheet of paper folded—

best like this, to go on
loving but not having, or having
but not knowing.

COLONIZATION

Does the devil use his tail as a weapon?
My son wants to know. He sees the abstract
made manifest—angular petal, red kite,
black heart on a cable. The heart itself
is an arrowhead, flint. Its point
is tangential, provocative, the brain's

vexation. No sparks today. Rain falls
so hard the drops ricochet in shattered
rings around the waterlogged worms—
crowns for the kings of the ground.
In the kitchen, an army of mildew
advances, trillions in gray-green

uniforms. The same invasion conquered
the trunk my mother brought back
from London in 1955, marched over
her clarinet concertos, her pink-tipped
reeds, colonized her letters. The blue
envelopes came, then stopped. Chameleon

on the rock of home, she lay barely
blinking in the Southern sun, her father
coughing sharp black specks
like the spores of a wart. She lay
like one of the dolls in the mineral
house he made—windows of mica,

asbestos pillows—Snow White
in transparent suspension, her mother

saying *go*. After the rain, the lilacs
smell sweet, then sweeter. They look
as lovely as yesterday, but their bruised
scent is making a different point.

BIRD OF PARADISE

It's not a bird, and that's part
of the problem. It calls into question
what pleases the eye, makes you doubt

what you see. If paradise means
things are what they seem, there's no need

for a second glance, or a second guess.

You can take what you want
and what you want
will want to be taken. But this flower,

if that's what it is, has more to do
with possibility than with paradise,

more to do with iron burning
in slow motion, smoldering orange dust.

You're in a church and that's part
of the problem. Vows aren't supposed to be
made with crossed fingers,

but you keep thinking of how he showed you
the configuration of a V-8 engine—

palms out, fingers laced together,
the way you'd turn your hands
into a church for a child, and say the rhyme.

God as an engine seems right. Not God
to make promises to, or in front of,

but God to grind promises up,

burn them like gas. You know
they must be good for something,

that they aren't meant to only be kept.

RECENT TITLES FROM ALICE JAMES BOOKS

ALICE JAMES BOOKS has been publishing exclusively poetry since 1973. One of the few presses in the country that is run collectively, the cooperative selects manuscripts for publication through both regional and national annual competitions. New regional authors become active members of the cooperative, participating in the editorial decisions of the press. The press, which historically has placed an emphasis on publishing women poets, was named for Alice James, sister of William and Henry, whose fine journal and gift for writing went unrecognized within her lifetime.

TYPESET AND DESIGNED BY DEDE CUMMINGS
& CAROLYN KASPER / DCDESIGN

PRINTED BY THOMSON-SHORE
ON 50% POSTCONSUMER RECYCLED PAPER
PROCESSED CHLORINE-FREE